JOIN THE BAND!

MARJORIE PILLAR

HarperCollins*Publishers*

IN MEMORY OF
Arlene M. Pillar
—the most loving taskmaster
anyone could have asked for.
She'll always have
a special place in my heart.

ACKNOWLEDGMENTS
Thanks to principal, staff,
and especially to the kids in the band
at Lloyd Harbor Elementary School.

And thanks to Ronnie Abrams,
for being my second pair of eyes!

Join the Band!
Copyright © 1992 by Marjorie Pillar
Printed in the U.S.A. All rights reserved.
1 2 3 4 5 6 7 8 9 10
First Edition

Library of Congress Cataloging-in-Publication Data
Pillar, Marjorie.
  Join the band! / by Marjorie Pillar.
    p. cm.
  Summary: A young musician describes the instruments of the school
band and the experience of participating in rehearsals and the
spring concert.
  ISBN 0-06-021834-7.—ISBN 0-06-021829-0 (lib. bdg.)
  1. Bands (Music)—Instruction and study—Juvenile. 2. Musical
instruments—Instruction and study—Juvenile. (1. Musical
instruments. 2. Bands (Music)) I. Title.
MT733.P6 1992   90-23261
784.4'4—dc20   CIP
                                                          AC   MN

All the photographs included in this book were
taken with Kodak Ektachrome 200 Professional Slide Film.

ASK any of us—the best thing about school is the band!
You can tell which kids are in the band by all their different instrument cases. My friends and I carry our instruments with us every day.

There are lots of great instruments
in our band: the trombone,
the drums, the trumpet,

the flute, the clarinet,
the saxophone, and
the French horn.

Mr. Meyer, our teacher, knows how to play them all.

For now, I'm learning just one instrument—the flute.

The whole band will play together in the spring concert. But first, we have a lot of practicing to do.

Before we can start, we have to get our instruments ready. The saxophone must be swabbed and the trumpet oiled.

The clarinet cork must be greased and the trombone sprayed.
I clean my flute with a soft cloth.

Some of the instruments have to be put together piece by piece.

The clarinet has the most parts of all—five!

Practice, practice, practice. That's what it takes for all of us to learn our parts. Mr. Meyer meets separately with each of the different instrument groups. It's great fun getting out of class for band practice!

Sometimes the trumpet players practice using only their mouthpieces. When they blow into them, the kids say their lips start to buzz.

The clarinetists finger their notes without blowing. If someone makes a mistake, no one can hear it!

If we can't figure out the music,
Mr. Meyer helps us. We keep trying.

It feels terrific when we finally get it right!

The whole band practices together two times a week. And we all practice at home every day, too. Mr. Meyer makes sure of that. He checks our practice charts every time we meet.

At the end of practice, we clean our instruments again and put them away.

You wouldn't believe how much we'll have practiced, preparing for our spring concert. Over one hundred hours! By early May, we're starting to sound ready.

We have a dress rehearsal on stage to get used to playing in the auditorium.

Finally, it's the night of the concert. The performance starts at 7:30. Just to be sure no one is late, Mr. Meyer wants *us* there at 6:00.

Everyone looks special tonight.
I can't believe it—two of my friends
are wearing the same dress!

As we wait to go on stage, we tune our instruments. Some of us practice together,

but some kids want to practice alone.

We fool around a lot because we're nervous. The noise gets so loud that we have to cover our ears. I wonder if they can hear us out front?

Time to go.
I hope I don't
forget my part.

This is it! Mr. Meyer gives the signal,

and the concert begins.

Amazing! We really
sound good together.

All of us work hard to do our best—even Mr. Meyer!

Before we know it, the concert is over.

The whole audience is clapping. We did it!

It's great to know that our friends and families really liked our music.

All that work, and it's over so fast. Now we can relax!

There's no doubt about it; school band is great. See for yourself—join the band!